being critical

. . .

kate williams

Blackwell's/Palgrave Study Guides

Pocket Study Skills

For a complete listing of all **Palgrave Study Skills** titles, please visit:
www.palgrave.com/studyskills

contents

introduction

The word 'critical' has several meanings in everyday life:

- finding fault: a negative comment such as *not good enough* / *sloppily done* / *could do better* / *why didn't you …?*
- key, decisive, crucial: as in *a critical moment* / *critically ill* / *a critical incident* / *a critical decision.*

Neither of these is the meaning of 'critical' when used to describe the quality lecturers want to see in students' writing at university: '*a critical approach*', '*critical analysis*', '*critical not descriptive writing*'.

This guide explains what 'being critical' means at university and shows how to achieve this quality in your work.

Many of the tips in this guide are developed in the Palgrave *Study Skills* and *Pocket Study Skills* series, so these may be your next step for more detailed advice.

Specific links are suggested at the bottom of the page throughout this guide, and are referred to by their title. Details are given on p22.

being 'critical' at university

Being critical is a mindset. For the most part, you already have it: you choose one phone deal / living arrangement / supermarket offer over another. You take into account one friend's recommendation but avoid another's favourite film. You do your research, discriminate, set one view against another.

Ultimately, make up your own mind about your position and take responsibility for your judgements. This is the mindset tutors want to see in your work. It shows in how you

- work out what you have to do (below)
- do your research and reading (Part 2)
- communicate the outcomes in your writing (Part 3)

1 Ask strategic questions

Asking questions right from the beginning is key to being critical in your work. Take those few moments before you dive into an assignment to clarify to yourself **what** exactly you are being asked to do and **how** you will set about it.

The six 'strategic questions' can help you with planning and the answers will help to bring your writing task into sharp focus. Read your course

---

For examples of essay and assignment planning, see *Planning your essay, Getting critical* Chs 1 and 10, *Planning your dissertation* Ch 1.

materials carefully and check and recheck online to make sure you have all the information and guidance available.

> ### *What* exactly are you being asked to produce?
>
> How is it described? Essay? Report? Assignment? Another specific format?
>
> What is the main topic? …the key aspects?
>
> Any guidance about structure / layout / style / length?
>
> What % marks does it count for?

> ### *Why* are you being asked to do this?
>
> Clearly, you must acquire the basic knowledge to understand the topic area. What is expected beyond this – to analyse? Apply? Look at the wording of the question, assessment criteria and learning outcomes.

> ### *Who* are you writing for?
>
> Your tutor is always your primary reader. What are they looking for?

> ### *How* will you do it?
>
> How will you research it? What theories / kinds of sources / practical activity?
> How will you write it? Is there an explicit instruction word?

> ### *When …?* and *Where …?* are the final questions which can kick-start you into critical thinking.

For more on the importance of instruction words, see *Planning your essay* Ch 4.

2 What tutors are looking for

The *Who?* question above will lead you to your reader. What do you know about what your reader / tutor expects and is looking for?

Tutors will *always* be looking for evidence of critical thinking and the evidence on which it is based.

For the specifics in each essay or assignment, check the **guidance** before you tackle the task, and **feedback** when it is returned and graded. Both are valuable sources for learning about the expectations of a particular tutor, and of the discipline you are studying.

Your analysis of the guidance should take you to the assessment criteria – however expressed. In assessment criteria tutors attempt both to describe the intellectual qualities they are looking for, and to explain subsequent grading.

Assessment criteria are often expressed in what can seem like abstract language, as tutors try to describe the 'quality' of critical thinking evidenced in writing. Read this guidance carefully and quiz it. Pick out the key phrases. For each, ask

• what does this mean?
• what do I have to DO to achieve it?

Feedback on returned work is valuable. However strong the temptation to look at the mark and shut your eyes, pick your moment to go through it carefully, noting tutor comments and reactions.

Quick reactions – ticks ✓or brief marginal notes: *Good point.* Your tutor likes this. What have you done right? Often it is where you show that you are thinking about what you have read, and make a comment, however brief, that shows you can see the relevance of it or connect it with other sources you refer to. This demonstrates a critical awareness.

For more on assessment and grades, see *Getting critical* Ch 2.

Longer comments are really valuable. They open up a conversation in which the tutor gives their comments on the subject you have written about AND offers 'reader reaction' to the overall impact of your writing.

Tutor comments often show what they expect critical writing to look like:

The question asks 'to what extent …? rather than 'whether'. You only offer a yes/no answer.

Whether the assignment title explicitly asks for it or not, you will almost always be expected to answer it as if it is a *'to what extent'* question. If there is a valid 'yes' or 'no' answer to the question, it probably would not be set! A thoughtful and critical student will know this, and will lead their reader through the assignment to their conclusion.

A *yes, but … no, but …* position shows the writer can see the complexity in the issues.

Very good analysis. You could go one step further and connect the analysis of the various issues: was the board unstable because of […] or did the problem arise because […]?

The advice to go *'one step further'* is pointing this student to the possible **implications** of their analysis, and how it **links** to the issues in (here) the case study. Beyond a good analysis are the *'So what? What next?'* questions – and the top grades.

3 Descriptive vs critical

This is rather descriptive. You need to be more critical.

Comments like this can be rather dispiriting: *What does s/he mean? What have I done wrong?*

It isn't 'wrong' to describe. It is a starting point.

Sometimes you are asked to describe an incident or process (*outline / explain / describe*). Here you show your ability to observe, record and retell. A good description shows you understand – the essential first step. This is often the first part of a task. You are then asked to analyse it, reflect on it, relate it to models or other accounts from sources you have read.

But if you ONLY describe what you have done / read / observed (unless the task expressly requires this), you are not taking the next critical step in using the material: showing how YOU analyse the themes in the topic, bring them together; weigh up the different contributions and show where YOU are in the discussion.

This is critical analysis where you analyse, compare and contrast; synthesise (bring together); evaluate; apply; justify. Most likely these and similar words appear in the higher grades of the assessment criteria.

Critical analytical thinking vs descriptive writing

Stella Cottrell (2013, p198) summarises some of the main differences between critical analytical and descriptive writing as follows. She also comments: *'students lose more marks for lack of critical analysis than for any other single weakness in their work'*. Take heed!

For an explanation of the terms used in assessment criteria, see *Getting critical* Chs 2 and 14.

Descriptive writing	Critical analytical writing
states what happened	identifies the significance
states what something is like	evaluates strengths and weaknesses
explains what a theory says	shows why something is relevant or suitable
explains how something works	indicates why something will work (best)
notes the methods used	identifies whether something is appropriate or suitable
says when something occurred	identifies why the timing is of importance
states the different components	weighs up the importance of component parts
states options	gives reasons for selecting each option
states links between items	shows the relevance of links between pieces of information

Adapted from Cottrell (2013) p198 with thanks

Look at the language! It tells you a lot …

Look at what the writer is doing in descriptive writing: *states / states / explains / explains / notes / says / states / states / states*. This tells me, the reader, that the writer has read the source (probably), but has nothing to say about it. They simply repeat what is there.

The writer in analytical writing is doing something much more active and the reader can see this: they *evaluate / show why / weigh up / give reasons for / make links*. It is clear they understand what they have read because they have thought about it and can use it. They are in control.

being critical in research and reading

A critical approach to research and reading starts before you have read anything …

Research starts with thinking – about

- what you have to do – the task you have been set (Part 1)
- what you know already
- where to start
- what sources you need to use

and then reading and making sense of what you read – and working out how you will (or will not) use it.

4   Where do I start?

First: what do you know already?

It is worth taking a few minutes to work this out.

Take a sheet of A4 and write the title of your task in the middle. Fill the rest of the sheet with jottings – questions arising from the question, the major topic areas, what you know and what you need to find out.

Identifying what you know will help you with your reading. It will point you to the gaps you need to fill, and the sorts of materials you should look for. Then it will help you connect with new material and link it to your existing knowledge. It will also help to keep you alert and questioning when you read.

Second: do the obvious

Start with the core materials of your course:

- lecture notes / slides / VLE materials
- week-by-week set readings – chapters, specific articles

This will give you the core knowledge in your subject and the foundation on which you can build. These are the essentials.

Third: choose carefully from the reading list

Take control and don't be intimidated by it!

You are not expected to read everything on a reading list. The longer it is, the more you are expected to be selective in what you read. Some suggestions are there to give you options – two or three different textbooks, for example. Others cluster into different topic areas to give some starting points for the different directions students may decide to go in in their research.

Fourth: use your reading list

Explore the websites, links and databases listed in your reading lists. These web sources will take you to the type and quality of information you should use in your research.

Starting research for an assignment with the set or recommended reading is common sense. It is also where you learn to be critical and scholarly, as these materials have been chosen as an introduction to the issues and debates in your subject. Your tutor will expect to see evidence that you have used these in your writing, and you can have confidence that you are on the right track.

For a critical approach to reading lists, see *Getting critical* Ch 4 and *Reading and making notes* Ch 6.

5 All sorts of sources

The reading list will take you to **books, journal articles, established websites** and **databases.** You will also be expected to go beyond the reading list and to decide for yourself what you will consult:

Government legislation *photos*
publications **catalogues** reviews
newspaper TV digital books
articles conference **blogs** **company reports**
radio papers **market research**
twitter **British** **(e.g. Mintel)** discussion
Standards advertisements groups

So – you're getting started. You will be the judge of everything you find. A critical approach means you will not be reading it because it's there or came up top in a Google search. Before you start reading, ask yourself:

- *what do I want to get out of reading this?*
- *what do I think the key points will be?* Note it down.

For a reading strategy, see *Reading and making notes* Chs 1 and 11.

A critical question: *Where am I?*
A couple of clicks from the most reputable of sources and you can be anywhere.

Web pages with no authors or dates **YouTube** single digital pages of books **more twitter** **Mrs McGee's advice** **Dr Bloomenschlicker of Wherizzit University** **lookalike sites ...**

All of life is out there in some form or other, and where there is life there is someone researching it. You, for example.

It's 'buyer beware!' Know where you are online – and use the strategic questions to quickly check it. The more gaps there are in the answers, and the less you can see of the context of the material you read, the more hesitant you should be about relying on it as evidence.

Be critical!

6   Is it relevant?

Just about anything can be relevant to your research. It all depends on the

- topic area you are researching and
- the question you are asking.

If your question is about the *opportunities and limitations of Twitter as a marketing tool,* you may decide to

- use specific tweets to illustrate a point
- draw on theory and studies on market segmentation and customer profiling to inform your points

You have to be clear about the purpose of the different sources, and show your research footprints through careful referencing.

This is being critical.

7 Is it reliable?

The concept of reliability is a tricky one. Guidance often suggests that there are 'good' sources and 'bad' sources. The reality is more complex.

The issue (see above) is about how you plan to use the material. If your question is about *whether there is a safe level of alcohol consumption for pregnant women*, you will find vast amounts of often conflicting information all over the web and social media. The debate could give you some interesting starting points. It could also give you a structure for your project.

You cannot assume, however, that the sources you find are of equal reliability. Just because it is there, doesn't mean it is true or that the research has been carried out meticulously. To establish this you need to know more about it and how it came to be. Quick check it with the strategic questions:

- **What** is it saying? Is it consistent with what you know from other sources?
- **Why** is it there?
- **Who** has produced the page / written the material? What are their credentials?
- **How** was the research carried out? Is the methodology clear? Is it logical in relation to the aims?
- **When**? How recent is it? How much does the date matter?
- **Where**? How relevant are results obtained in this location/situation to yours?

If you want to rely on a source as evidence, you need to be confident that the evidence is sound. This will lead you to reliable sources, including articles in peer-reviewed journals as evidence for the points or arguments you make. These have been checked in detail by other researchers in the field and so have been through the quality assurance process in the academic world.

A critical question: *Where am I?*

Are you looking at the research itself, or someone else reporting on it?

Primary sources are written or collated by the person or organisation that carried out the work themselves, at first hand: data collection, case study, company report, theory. An article by the researcher(s) who carried out the study themselves is considered to be a primary source.

Secondary sources are written by someone who has read the primary material and described or summarised it in some way. A textbook or article that refers to or summarises other studies is a secondary source. It's a good place to start.

If you only use secondary sources like a textbook in your work, you will only see the aspects of the study that the writer of the secondary source chooses to include. If you really want to know what the original source said, you need to find and read it yourself.

Be critical!

So – you read it. Think back over it:

- *Did you get what you wanted from it?* Look back at your brief notes.
- *Can you summarise the key points?* Try and capture it in a few bullets.

Decision time

Critical thinking does not stop with finding a robust article. You have to decide

- will you use it in your assignment? is it ***relevant?***
- and if you do, ***how?***
- what the implications are for your argument, or what you want to say: the critical ***so what?***

It's time to move on to planning and writing.

For how to reference secondary sources, see *Referencing and understanding plagiarism* Ch 14.

3

being critical in writing

You write throughout your research – thoughts, plans, notes on your reading. It helps you think. But don't confuse the writing-as-you-go with writing the assignment you have to hand in.

This is different. Here you plan how you will pull it all together. Before you rush to hit the keys, pause, step back, step up and look at the bigger picture.

- Where does your research (your new **knowledge** and **understanding**) fit in with what you have been asked to investigate? (the **question**)
- How does it inform your thinking about it? (your **analysis**)
- How will you communicate this to your reader? (your **organisation** and **structure**)

Part 3 sets out the steps to achieve this.

Start here:

> First
> **Analyse the question**
> Then …

For practical advice on how to analyse the question, see *Planning your essay* Ch 4 and *Getting critical* Ch 10.

8 Plan your answer

Have you noticed how often assignment tasks are referred to as 'the question'? Often there is no question mark in sight, and the task is long and looks like a TO DO list of areas you have to jigsaw together – yet it is referred to as 'the question'.

Hidden under any title is **always a question**: *what is your position on this? To what extent [do you think] this is the case? How convincing [do you think] the evidence is [or is not] that ...?* If there does not appear to be a question in your 'question' look at it carefully and try and find a hidden question. It will help you plan your answer.

Planning is where you take control of the assignment and make it your own. It is where you map out the points you want to make. This framework will ensure that your writing is a live communication with a real and interested reader who wants to know what you make of it all.

9 Write for your reader

Your reader/tutor is interested in what you take away from your learning and reading, remember? Don't bore them by telling them what they know already (*Boogleschiffer 2012 states that ...*), but engage them in what YOU have to say.

Use your structure to make it easy for them to see your line of development or reasoning. Imagine they only read the first sentence of each paragraph. Can they see where you are going?

For practical advice, see
Planning your essay Ch 5
Getting critical Ch 10 and
Planning your dissertation Ch 13.

From point to paragraph to argument

Each point in your plan becomes a paragraph in your writing. Each paragraph starts with a topic sentence in which the writer makes their point. Each paragraph is a step in your argument.

Below are four paragraphs from Fede's essay:

How effective has PEPFAR been as a bilateral approach to combating HIV/AIDS?

> *Bilateral aid programmes are those from which resources are channelled directly from one government to another, as opposed to …*

- Fede's point is to **distinguish between** one form of aid and another.
- The definition shows research and **understanding** (well summarised).
- *As opposed to* … points to **analysis** to follow.

> *It falls upon Congress to approve any new funds that USAID wishes to disburse, which critics argue allows for political, moral, commercial and religious interests to influence … (Biddell 2010; Muller et al. 2012) …*

- The writer clearly knows about the role of Congress (**knowledge** and **understanding** from research)
- … and the debates that surround it: the paragraph will be about what the critics say about it. This moves swiftly to **analysis, synthesis** of different sources and points to evaluation to come.

> *It was not only faith-based interests that found their way into PEPFAR: commercial interests also influenced …*

- The writer can be seen weighing up the different elements. It's no longer a list of influences, but the writer can be seen thinking: *how influential is each element in this?* This is **evaluation**.

The outline above illustrates the steps in the *Stairway to critical thinking* in *Getting critical* Chs 3 and 14.

> *The question of the effectiveness of aid has become increasingly pressing recently. Diverse donors have entered the aid arena …*
>
> • The writer is moving to a new (related) area in which he considers where the debates impact on practice. This is **application** – where he addresses the ***so what?*** question of why the debates matter in combating HIV/AIDS.

Adapted, with thanks

And yes, from these topic sentences the reader can clearly see the development of the writer's argument, paragraph by paragraph.

10 Writing skills for critical writing

Show the reader each source as soon as you start to draw on it

Don't leave your reader to puzzle over whose ideas they are reading or whose 'voice' they are hearing. YOU have a voice, a style, a perspective. This is different to the style, language and content of a source. Make sure you show which is which immediately by introducing the reference at the point you start to draw on that source. For example:

Building local capacity is crucial to […], because, as noted by Dumont et al. (2011), the impacts of AIDS range from the immediate to the very long-term and …

The reader can see the writer's voice in his point (about building local capacity), and that he summarises a point made by Dumont et al. The reference to the source of an idea is not just about quoting words – it's about acknowledging ideas.

The reader wants to 'hear' the 'voices':

A reader asks: *Who made this point? What did you have to do to know it?*

The writer answers: *I found and read Dumont et al's article.*

By positioning the reference immediately, you answer the reader's question before they have (grumpily) asked it. If you place a reference at the end of a chunk of writing, the reader can't see where you are making your point and where you draw on another researcher's work. This does not show critical awareness. You run the risk of looking as if you have just copied and pasted material from somewhere else.

Use the right word to introduce your sources
- **to show you can see what other writers do in their text**

Showing you can see what another writer is doing tells your reader that you are in control of your sources and appreciate what each writer is doing in their text. In the example above, Dumont et al. (2011) *noted* ... An author may be doing other things:

- *identifies X, Y and Z as major causes of ...*
- *uses examples of [...] as evidence that ...*
- *questions whether ...*
- *traces the development of ...*
- *defines ... as ...*

In one word you can show your critical awareness, reflected in your writing.

- **to show your position in relation to what another writer says or is doing**

This is a fundamental skill in conveying your argument and will lift your writing from being merely 'descriptive' to being critical, analytical and evaluative.

Try using verbs like these:

- points out ...
- argues ...
- maintains ...
- claims ...
- suggests ...
- concludes ...

Adapted from University of Manchester (2015)

Careful choice of verbs to introduce a source can signal doubt ('claims'), caution ('suggests'), a point of specific interest ('points out') and so on. Just by using the right word you can signal your position, lift your writing from being an account to an argument, and ensure that you are never simply describing. You are always showing your critical awareness.

Avoid words that lead you into description

Do you use – or overuse – verbs like *says / states / highlights / looks at / according to*?
Telling your reader what each author said on the subject will lead you into descriptive writing. Where's the added-value of your thinking?

Sometimes these introductory verbs are appropriate: *The government states that Pupil Premium Funding has increased year on year* (DfE 2013, updated 2014).

The reader is now expecting a comment: … *however, Head Teachers argue that the increase does not reflect …* Here the writer uses the neutral introduction to lead into discussion. Without discussion it is just … err … what some author or organisation said. Where's the analysis?

Can I say *I think / in my opinion / I believe*?

These should be used sparingly and in most cases not at all. If you use these phrases, your reader might think you lack

- awareness: of other practitioners or readings
- criticality: have you thought about it? Questioned it?
- rigour: have you checked that it is well founded?

For more on the language of argument, see *Planning your dissertation* Ch 19 and *Writing for university* Chs 14–16.

Or you could come across as arrogant – something is right simply because you believe it to be! If you take off *I think* / *I believe* you are just left with an opinion however sincerely held. Without any reference to research or other evidence it is just … an assertion, showing no critical awareness of the complexity of the issue.

Use linking words

Careful use of the right words to signpost your reader through your writing helps to create a logical flow of ideas (as in the extract on pp15–16). It makes your writing easier and more enjoyable to read because as a reader you can anticipate what comes next.

You create an expectation that you are going to

- add another similar point: *Similarly … / Furthermore … / not only … but also*
- move to a contrasting point: *conversely / in contrast / as opposed to*
- restate: *that is to say / put simply*

Your writing not only flows better, but by signalling what is coming next, the reader can follow how you have organised your ideas.

Linking words also help to show the connections between ideas:

- signal a different direction: *however / nevertheless / although / despite*
- continue in the same direction: *equally / furthermore / similarly*

Used carefully, the choice of the right linking words can strengthen the sense the reader has of a thoughtful, critical writer.

For more on using 'I' and 'we', see *Writing for university* Ch 15 and *Reflective writing* pp67–69.

11 Conclusions and introductions

Use your conclusion to show where all that critical thinking, planning and writing has taken you.

Try structuring it like this:

- State where you got to in your thinking and research on the question; your conclusions, take-away points for your reader.
- Sum up what you covered.
- Show what this means for the 'bigger picture' or the topic of your essay.

Now write (or rewrite) the introduction

Now you know exactly where you ended, you are in a position to write your introduction. You know you can deliver on your promise because you have just done it! Try this for a structure:

- Introduce the 'bigger picture': the topic / context / issue / debates.
- Show the angle you will be exploring (your argument).
- Outline your main points.

A clear and logical structure makes it easier for you to write, and for your reader to follow your argument.

Becoming critical

This guide has focused on showing the interconnections between many of the aspects of being critical in your written work.

For more signposting and linking words, see *Writing for university* Ch 17 and *Planning your essay* Ch 17.

For how to structure an introduction, see *Planning your essay* Ch 6 and *Planning your dissertation* Ch 22.

What is that critical thing? I hope you can see that it is a **mindset** you bring to your work and a **set of skills** you employ. Use them to show your critical awareness in your 'voice' as a writer from start to finish.

Enjoy!

References

Cottrell S (2013). *The study skills handbook* (4th edition). Basingstoke: Palgrave Macmillan.

Manchester University Library (2014). Being critical: thinking, reading and writing critically. Critical writing strategy: It says / I say / and so. Available at www.escholar.manchester.ac.uk/learning-objects/mle/being-critical/ [Accessed 27 February 2015].

University of Manchester (2015). *Academic phrasebank*. Available at www.phrasebank.manchester.ac.uk/referring-to-sources/ [Accessed 4 March 2015].

Linked books in the *Palgrave Study Skills* and *Pocket Study Skills* series

Cottrell S (2011). *Critical thinking skills: developing effective analysis and argument* (2nd edition). Basingstoke: Palgrave Macmillan.

Godfrey J (2014). *Reading and making notes* (2nd edition). Basingstoke: Palgrave Macmillan.

Godfrey J (2011). *Writing for university*. Basingstoke: Palgrave Macmillan.

Godwin J (2014). *Planning your essay* (2nd edition). Basingstoke: Palgrave Macmillan.

Williams K (2014). *Getting critical* (2nd edition). Basingstoke: Palgrave Macmillan.

Williams K (2013). *Planning your dissertation*. Basingstoke: Palgrave Macmillan.

Williams K and Carroll J (2009). *Referencing and understanding plagiarism*. Basingstoke: Palgrave Macmillan.

Williams K, Woolliams M and Spiro J (2012). *Reflective writing*. Basingstoke: Palgrave Macmillan.

POCKET STUDY SKILLS
Kate Williams

GETTING CRITICAL

SECOND EDITION

---

www.skills4study.com

PALGRAVE STUDY SKILLS

BY THE ½ MILLION COPY BESTSELLING AUTHOR
SECOND EDITION

CRITICAL THINKING SKILLS

DEVELOPING EFFECTIVE ANALYSIS AND ARGUMENT

STELLA COTTRELL

POCKET STUDY SKILLS

WRITING
FOR
UNIVERSITY

Jeanne Godfrey

POCKET STUDY SKILLS

PLANNING
YOUR
ESSAY

SECOND EDITION

Janet Godwin

POCKET STUDY SKILLS

REFLECTIVE
WRITING

Kate Williams, Mary Woolliams and Jane Spiro

POCKET STUDY SKILLS
Kate Williams & Jude Carroll

REFERENCING & UNDERSTANDING PLAGIARISM

PALGRAVE STUDY SKILLS

NINTH EDITION

CITE THEM RIGHT

THE ESSENTIAL REFERENCING GUIDE

RICHARD PEARS
GRAHAM SHIELDS

POCKET STUDY SKILLS

PLANNING YOUR DISSERTATION

Kate Williams

PALGRAVE STUDY SKILLS

DISSERTATIONS AND PROJECT REPORTS

A STEP BY STEP GUIDE

STELLA COTTRELL

First published 2015 by
PALGRAVE

Palgrave in the UK is an imprint of Macmillan Publishers Limited, registered in England, company number 785998, of 4 Crinan Street, London, N1 9XW.

Palgrave Macmillan in the US is a division of St Martin's Press LLC, 175 Fifth Avenue, New York, NY 10010.

Palgrave is a global imprint of the above companies and is represented throughout the world.

Palgrave® and Macmillan® are registered trademarks in the United States, the United Kingdom, Europe and other countries.

ISBN: 978-1-137-54753-8   paperback

This book is printed on paper suitable for recycling and made from fully managed and sustained forest sources. Logging, pulping and manufacturing processes are expected to conform to the environmental regulations of the country of origin.

A catalogue record for this book is available from the British Library.